D0609391

curious
NATURE

Q & A
ABOUT

BIOMES

NANCY DICKMANN

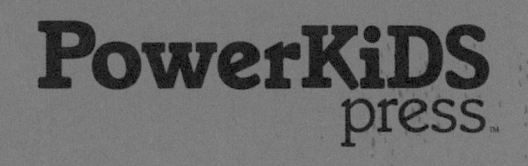

PowerKiDS
press

Published in 2018 by **The Rosen Publishing Group, Inc.**
29 East 21st Street, New York, NY 10010

Cataloging-in-Publication Data
Names: Dickmann, Nancy.
Title: Q & A about biomes / Nancy Dickmann.
Description: New York : PowerKids Press, 2018. | Series: Curious nature | Includes index.
Identifiers: ISBN 9781499433913 (pbk.) | ISBN 9781499433852 (library bound) | ISBN 9781499433739 (6 pack)
Subjects: LCSH: Biotic communities--Juvenile literature.
Classification: LCC QH541.14 D54 2018 | DDC 577--dc23

For Brown Bear Books Ltd:
Text and Editor: Nancy Dickmann
Editorial Director: Lindsey Lowe
Children's Publisher: Anne O'Daly
Design Manager: Keith Davis
Designer and Illustrator: Supriya Sahai
Picture Manager: Sophie Mortimer
Concept development: Square and Circus/Brown Bear Books Ltd

Picture Credits: All photographs copyright Shutterstock.

Brown Bear Books has made every attempt to contact the copyright holder.
If anyone has any information please contact licensing@brownbearbooks.co.uk

Manufactured in the United States of America

CPSIA Compliance Information: Batch BS17PK: For Further Information contact Rosen Publishing, New York, New York at 1-800-237-9932.

CONTENTS

WHAT IS A BIOME?

Our amazing planet has tall mountains and dry deserts. There are forests, grasslands, and the icy poles. All of these places are biomes. A biome is a large area with similar weather and land. It is home to plants and animals. They are suited to the biome's conditions.

Every biome is different. Some are rainy and some are dry. Some are hot and some are cold. They may have rich soil, or they may be rocky or sandy. Not all biomes are on land. Rivers and oceans are biomes, too.

CHANGING BIOMES

Sometimes people change biomes. We plow prairies and plant crops there. We build dams across rivers. We cut down forests. These changes affect the plants and animals that live in a biome. They can make it harder for the plants and animals to survive.

ADAPTATIONS

Plants and animals have adaptations. These are features that help them survive in their biomes. A polar bear could not survive in a tropical rain forest. But its thick fur and big paws are perfect for living in the snow.

HOW DO ANIMALS LIVE IN DESERTS?

All animals need water to live. But it's hard to find water in a desert. Deserts are dry and can be very hot. Desert animals need to be smart about finding water and keeping cool.

Many animals get their water from food. They eat cactuses, insects, and seeds. Some spend the day in underground burrows. It is cooler there. They come out at dawn and dusk to feed.

Cactuses can store water in their thick stems.

COLD DESERTS

We think of deserts as hot, but some are cold. In China's Gobi Desert, snow can fall during the winter. Few plants grow there.

Thick eyelashes keep sand out of its eyes. Its nostrils can close to keep sand out, too.

HOW A CAMEL SURVIVES IN THE DESERT

The **hump** contains fat. This acts as an energy source. It lets the camel go for a long time without eating or drinking.

Camels eat prickly desert plants. Their **thick lips** don't get hurt by the spines.

When **water** is available, a camel can drink 30 gallons (136 l) in just 13 minutes.

A camel's **large, flat feet** keep it from sinking into the sand.

7

IS A RAIN FOREST REALLY RAINY?

Tropical rain forests grow in places that are hot and wet. Most get at least 100 inches (2.5 m) of rain every year. Some get more than 300 inches (8 m)!

More types of plants and animals live in rain forests than in any other biome. Some animals live in the tall trees. Others live on the ground.

Sloths move slowly through the trees, eating leaves.

COOL RAIN FORESTS

Some forests are rainy but cool. Many of the trees have needles instead of leaves. Mosses and ferns grow there, too. These cool rain forests are often found near the coast.

The **tallest trees** spread wide to catch the sun's light. Birds, bats, and butterflies fly through this layer.

The **canopy** is a thick layer of leaves and branches. They block rain and sun, making the layers below darker. Sloths, monkeys, and insects eat fruits in the canopy.

Shorter plants live below the canopy. Their big leaves catch as much light as possible. Tree frogs, snakes, and jaguars live here.

It is dark and damp on the **forest floor**. Small animals break down the leaves that fall here.

WHO LIVES IN A ROTTEN LOG?

Not all forests are rainy. Deciduous forests cover many parts of the world. Their trees are green and leafy. Bears, deer, raccoons, and foxes live in these forests. So do owls and woodpeckers.

When old trees die, they fall down. New trees grow to replace them. The dead trees provide food and homes for living things.

Woodpeckers use their beaks to find insects inside trees.

WINTER IN THE FOREST

In the winter, the trees have no leaves. There is less food for the forest animals. Some of them sleep through the winter. This is called hibernation. It helps the animals save energy.

The wood in a rotting log is full of nutrients.
When it decays, the nutrients are recycled.
Other living things can now use them.

Moss grows well on a dead log.

Fungi grow on the dead log. They get their food from the rotting wood.

A rotting log is a perfect home for **centipedes**. They like to live in damp, sheltered spaces.

Small animals such as **salamanders** live in the hollow log.

Termites and other insects eat the dead wood. They break it down and help it turn back into soil.

11

WHY DO PINE TREES HAVE NEEDLES?

Coniferous trees do not lose their leaves in winter. Their leaves are shaped like needles. They stay green all year round. These trees are often found in cold places.

A lot of snow falls in winter. The snow slides off the needles. In the winter, the ground freezes. The trees can't take in water through their roots. The needles have a thick, waxy coating. It helps them keep water in.

Trees with needles produce cones with seeds hidden inside.

TYPES OF NEEDLES

Some trees have long, thin needles. They grow in small **bundles.**

Some trees have needles arranged in a **cluster.**

Some trees have soft, **flat needles**. They grow on both sides of a branch.

Some trees have fans of **scaly** needles.

Some trees' needles make a **spiral** pattern around the branch.

FOREST NAMES

Trees with needles grow in huge forests. They grow in the northern part of the Earth. The forests have different names. They can be called boreal forest, snow forest, or taiga.

DO PRAIRIE DOGS HELP THE SOIL?

Grasslands have tall grasses and few trees. Temperate grasslands have warm summers and cold winters. In North America, they are called prairies. They are called steppes in Europe and Central Asia.

Bison, deer, birds, and prairie dogs live in prairies. Prairie dogs dig tunnels under the ground. The tunnels help mix up the soil. They allow air to flow through. They help rain go down into the soil. This helps plants grow.

Huge bison graze on prairie grasses.

FARMING

Prairies often have rich soil. It is good for growing crops, so many prairies have been turned into farmland. Plants are dug up, and animals must find new homes. People are working hard to help save the prairies.

Some prairie grasses grow tall. They die back in the winter.

Prairie chickens build nests in the tall grass.

Prairie plants have deep roots. The plants die back in the winter. In the spring, they grow back from the roots.

Burrowing owls sometimes share the prairie dogs' homes.

Prairie dogs have big burrows. There are lots of "rooms." Some are used as toilets. Others are used as bedrooms. Some are used for raising babies.

HOW DO BUSHFIRES START?

Grasslands in warm places are called savannas. They are covered in grasses. They also have small shrubs and some trees. There are savannas in Africa, South America, and Australia.

Savannas are often hit by bushfires. Lightning can start fires, especially when it is hot and dry. People start some fires, either by accident or on purpose. Savanna grasses have deep roots. They can grow again after a fire.

Acacia trees need very little rain.

Bushfires can burn for days, destroying homes and habitats.

Leopards hide in the grass as they hunt.

16

RAINY AND DRY

Savannas are warm all year round. They have two main seasons: rainy and dry. When rain falls, flowers bloom and the savanna springs to life. In the dry season, animals go to water holes to find water.

Tiny **termites** build huge mounds.

Giraffes use their long necks to reach the top branches of acacia trees. Their long tongues pick the leaves.

Impala feed on the savanna's grasses.

Elephants eat tree bark. They also eat grasses, leaves, and fruit.

17

WHO LIVES IN EARTH'S COLDEST PLACES?

The area near the North Pole is called the Arctic. The land around the South Pole is called Antarctica. These places stay cold all year. The land is covered with snow and ice. Ice even covers the surface of the ocean!

Seals, walruses, and killer whales live in the polar oceans. They have a thick layer of fat called "blubber." It keeps their bodies warm. Reindeer and polar bears have thick fur to protect them from the cold.

TUNDRA
The weather gets slightly warmer as you travel away from the poles. This landscape is called tundra. It is warm enough for plants to grow in the summer. There are grasses and small shrubs, but no trees.

Walruses use their tusks to make holes in the ice.

EMPEROR PENGUIN CHICKS

Emperor penguins breed in Antarctica. In spring, they leave the water and walk to their nesting ground.

The female penguin lays an egg. She carefully passes it to the male.

Then she goes back to the ocean to hunt. The male puts the egg on his feet and covers it with his stomach. This keeps the egg warm.

It is the middle of winter. The male penguins huddle together to keep warm. There is nothing for them to eat.

The females return when the eggs hatch. Now the male can go find food.

19

WHY DON'T TREES GROW ON TALL MOUNTAINS?

The tallest mountains have no trees at the top. There is just snow or ice here. Trees cannot grow if it is too cold or dry. The higher you go up a mountain, the colder it gets. Mountains have an imaginary line called the "timberline." It marks the highest place where trees can grow.

It is hard for animals to survive on tall mountains. Some mountain animals hibernate in the winter. Others move down the mountain.

Mountain goats can climb steep, rocky slopes without slipping.

MOUNTAIN ZONES

Nothing can grow right at the top. The rocks are covered with snow and ice.

MOUNTAIN PLANTS
Plants that live high on mountains grow close to the ground. This protects them from wind. They have a chemical inside that keeps them from freezing. Their small leaves keep them from losing too much water.

Only small plants and shrubs grow above the timberline. They can cope with cold weather and little water.

TIMBERLINE

Conifers (trees with needles) can grow higher up the mountain slopes.

It is fairly warm and wet on the lower slopes. **Deciduous** trees grow here.

WHO LIVES IN FRESHWATER?

The water in the oceans is salty. Water in lakes and rivers is not. It is called freshwater. Humans and many other animals can only drink freshwater. Most water plants and animals can live in freshwater or in salt water, but not both.

The water in rivers is always flowing. Plants and animals in rivers must cope with a moving habitat! Fish swim in rivers. Other animals, such as otters or wading birds, live on the banks.

Bull sharks can live in salt water or freshwater.

WATERBIRDS

Rivers, lakes, and ponds are home to many birds. Kingfishers live near rivers. They perch on branches until they see a fish. Then they dive in to catch it.

Rushes have flexible stems. They bend gently in the flowing water, but do not break.

LIFE IN A RIVER

Plants such as algae use root-like parts to hold onto rocks.

When they are not feeding, crayfish hide under rocks to avoid the current.

Small fish have a streamlined shape. It lets the water flow easily past them.

WHAT IS THE MIDNIGHT ZONE?

Oceans cover about 70 percent of the Earth's surface. There are three main layers, or zones. The sunlit zone is at the top. It gets the sun's light during the day. Most of the oceans' plants and animals live here.

The deeper you go, the darker it gets. Only a little light reaches the twilight zone. The midnight zone is the deepest part. It is very cold here. Deep-sea animals have adapted to live in total darkness.

Anglerfish use their glowing light to lure animals to eat.

MAKING LIGHT

Some ocean creatures make their own light. Chemicals in their bodies make them glow. Some use light to catch prey or scare enemies away. Others use it to find a mate.

OCEAN ZONES

Tiny plants float in the **sunlit zone.** They provide food for sea animals. Sea turtles, fish, sharks, and corals live in the sunlit zone.

It is colder and darker in the **twilight zone.** Sperm whales dive down to find food. Sponges, octopuses, and squid live here.

There is no light in the **midnight zone.** Many of the animals here don't have eyes. Gulper eels, anglerfish, and brittle stars live here.

WHICH TREES CAN GROW UNDERWATER?

Wetlands are places where the ground is very wet. Sometimes they are covered with water. Freshwater wetlands have different names. Marshes and swamps are wetlands. So are bogs and fens. Freshwater wetlands sometimes form near rivers and streams.

Wetlands also form on coasts. The water is salty. It rises and falls with the tides. Mangrove trees grow here. They have special features that help them survive.

Some wetlands are home to alligators.

Egrets and other birds come to find food.

USEFUL MANGROVES

Mangroves help to protect the coasts from ocean waves. They provide homes for many animals. People often cut down mangroves. They want to use the land for other things. We need to protect mangroves.

A MANGROVE SWAMP

Some mangroves get rid of extra salt. It comes out through their leaves.

Roots above ground keep the tree stable.

Mangrove roots can take in air. Some poke up above the water's surface. Others have tiny breathing holes. They close up when covered by water.

Fish, crabs, and other shellfish live in the shelter of the roots.

27

MAKE A BIOME

Every biome needs plants. They take in water from the soil and release it into the air. You can make your own biome. Then watch it to see how it grows!

WHAT YOU NEED

* large glass container (such as a fishbowl, vase, or pickle jar)
* small stones
* a few larger stones for decoration
* potting soil
* small plant seedlings (such as ivy and ferns, which grow well in damp air)
* moss

1 Clean the glass container. Put a layer of small stones about 1 inch (3 cm) deep at the bottom.

2 Add potting soil until the container is half full.

Do not put your biome in direct sunlight.

3 Plant the seedlings carefully in the soil. Put the biggest ones in the middle.

4 Add moss, large stones, and other decorations.

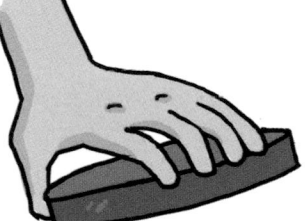

NOT TOO WET

Do the sides and top of your biome get misty in bright light? If so, you have the right amount of water. If there is no moisture on the sides, you need to add water. If the sides are always very wet, there is too much water. Take the lid off for a few hours.

5 Water the plants, but not too much. Then put the lid on. You can also use plastic wrap to cover the top.

GLOSSARY

adaptation change in a living thing that helps it survive where it lives

biome large area that has the same weather, land features, and plants

breed come together to have babies

conifer tree with leaves shaped like needles

crops plants that are grown for food

current area of moving water in a river or ocean

deciduous tree tree that loses its leaves each winter

desert area of land where very little rain falls

dusk time of day just before night

grassland large area of land covered by grass

habitat place where a plant or animal lives

North Pole imaginary point on Earth's surface that marks the farthest northern place

prairie type of grassland found in North America and other places

root part of a plant that grows below ground

South Pole imaginary point on Earth's surface that marks the farthest southern place

streamlined having a smooth, sleek shape that moves easily through air or water

survive continue to live

swamp wetland that is sometimes covered with water, where trees grow

tropical having a warm climate

FURTHER RESOURCES

BOOKS

Boothroyd, Jennifer. *Let's Visit the Deciduous Forest.* Lightning Bolt Books Biome Explorers. Minneapolis, MN: Lerner Publications: 2016.

Bow, James. *Grasslands Inside Out.* Ecosystems Inside Out. St. Catharines, ON: Crabtree Publishing Company, 2014.

Rizzo, Johnna. *Ocean Animals: Who's Who in the Deep Blue.* Washington, DC: National Geographic Children's Books, 2016.

Waldron, Melanie. *Polar Regions.* Habitat Survival. Chicago: Heinemann-Raintree, 2012.

WEBSITES

Due to the changing nature of Internet links, PowerKids Press has developed an online list of websites related to the subject of this book. This site is updated regularly.

Please use this link to access the list:
www.powerkidslinks.com/cn/biomes

INDEX